FlashRevise
Pocketbook

AS Economics

Philip Allan Updates, an imprint of Hodder Education, an Hachette UK company, Market Place, Deddington, Oxfordshire OX15 0SE

Orders

Bookpoint Ltd, 130 Milton Park, Abingdon, Oxfordshire OX14 4SB

tel: 01235 827720   fax: 01235 400454   e-mail: uk.orders@bookpoint.co.uk

Lines are open 9.00 a.m.–5.00 p.m., Monday to Saturday, with a 24-hour message answering service. You can also order through our website: www.philipallan.co.uk

© Philip Allan Updates 2009

ISBN 978-1-4441-0185-0

First published in 2004 as *Flashrevise Cards*

Impression number   5   4   3   2   1
Year   2014   2013   2012   2011   2010   2009

Printed in Spain

Hachette UK's policy is to use papers that are natural, renewable and recyclable products and made from wood grown in sustainable forests. The logging and manufacturing processes are expected to conform to the environmental regulations of the country of origin.

P01558

The economic problem

Q1 Economics is the study of how s............... resources are allocated.

Q2 Identify two allocative mechanisms.

Q3 If useful natural resources do not require an allocative mechanism, what are they called?

Q4 Explain a situation in which fresh air would be an economic good.

ANSWERS

the situation in which there are not
enough resources available to satisfy
all human needs and wants

A1 *scarce* — the fundamental economic problem is the need to allocate resources that are scarce

A2 • the price mechanism
• command or central direction

A3 free goods — e.g. air and solar energy, which are useful goods whose supply cannot be controlled

A4 if air became so polluted that people had to pay to consume fresh air

***examiner's* note** It is important to recognise that:
• There is a difference between the economic problem and issues such as inflation and unemployment, which are symptoms of the underlying problem.
• Free goods are not goods provided free by government, which are, of course, economic goods.
• In economics, all products that require an allocative mechanism are termed scarce.

1 **ANSWERS**

Scarcity and choice

Q1 Is water that you can drink a scarce resource?

Q2 Consumers who are faced with scarce products have a scale of preference that requires them to choose those products that give most s_____ per unit of m_____ spent.

Q3 Is heat always and everywhere a scarce resource?

Q4 What are the three basic questions in economics?

ANSWERS ▶▶

scarce resources make it necessary for producers and consumers to exercise choice

A1 yes, if the water requires treatment to make it fit to drink and there are private ownership rights

A2 *satisfaction; money*

A3 no, not in those countries where it is available naturally as a free good

A4 what to produce, how to produce and for whom to produce

***examiner's* note** The preference a consumer has for various products is relatively easy to identify based upon the choices they make. It is, however, impossible to value one person's preferences against those of another person in any scientific way. This means that theories of consumer behaviour are relatively unrealistic. Nevertheless, they do help us to understand the basic concepts of scarcity and choice.

Opportunity cost

Q1 Opportunity cost is a r............ measure of value.

Q2 What is the opportunity cost of producing more capital goods at a level of full employment?

Q3 If a carpenter could produce three chairs or two tables, what would be the opportunity cost of producing one chair?

Q4 Is there an opportunity cost of providing a free national health service? Explain.

ANSWERS ▶▶

A1 *real* — a measure in terms of another product, and not a nominal measure in money

A2 producing fewer consumer goods

A3 1 chair = $\dfrac{2 \text{ (tables)}}{3 \text{ (chairs)}} = \frac{2}{3}$ table

A4 yes; there is no opportunity cost of consuming the product, but there is an opportunity cost of producing health services

***examiner's* note** Opportunity cost is a very important concept in economics as it is used to explain both the advantages of labour specialisation and internal trade, as well as the gains from international trade. It can be measured in terms of what is forgone by the consumer or what is given up by the producer when resources are used in a particular way. Only free goods have no opportunity cost.

Production possibility boundary

Q1 Why is this function called a boundary?

Q2 Describe the relationship between X and Y along the boundary.

Q3 What does point A suggest about productive capacity?

Q4 What is the difference between points B and C?

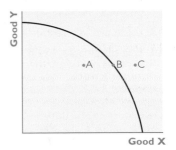

ANSWERS

A1 given scarce resources and current technology, this represents the limits, or boundary, for producing various combinations of good X and good Y

A2 it is only possible to produce more of X if less of Y is produced and vice versa

A3 there are idle resources and productive capacity is not fully utilised

A4 B is obtainable, while C is unobtainable

***examiner's* note** Production possibility boundaries are used in both macro and microeconomics to illustrate the limits to production, given fully employed resources. All points inside the boundary are achievable, but they are not utilising resources efficiently as there is the possibility of increasing the output along both axes by moving to the boundary. A variety of alternative names are used to describe the production possibility boundary — these include production possibility curve, production possibility frontier and product transformation curve.

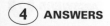

ANSWERS

Shifting production possibility boundaries

Q1 Why are these boundaries convex?

Q2 What is the cause of a shift from XY to X_1Y_1?

Q3 What is the opportunity cost of producing X_2 of capital goods?

Q4 Is a change in quantity produced from X_3 to X_2 or from Y_2 to Y_3 more likely to shift the boundary?

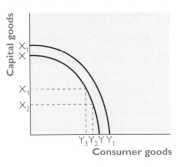

ANSWERS

A1 there is likely to be a most efficient combination of capital and consumer goods produced, so there is a diminishing marginal rate of substitution

A2 a growth in productive capacity

A3 if X_2 of capital goods is produced, then either $X - X_2$ of capital goods or $Y - Y_2$ of consumer goods cannot be produced

A4 from Y_2 to Y_3; a fall in the quantity of consumer goods produced means that more capital goods can be produced and this is more likely to cause a growth in capacity

***examiner's* note** It is a common mistake in examinations to read the opportunity cost of producing on one axis as what is produced on the other axis, rather than what is *not* produced on *either* axis. In addition, any movement from inside a production possibility boundary towards the boundary produces a growth in output, but it should not be confused with economic growth, which is illustrated by a shift in the boundary.

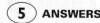

(**5**) **ANSWERS**

Efficiency

Q1 Why is capitalism thought to be a more efficient way of allocating resources than communism?

Q2 Is it possible for a firm to be productively efficient and making a loss? Explain your answer.

Q3 How can a firm become more efficient over time?

Q4 What is Pareto efficiency?

ANSWERS ▸▸

the ratio of useful work done to total energy expended

A1 market forces are more responsive to economic needs and wants than centralised bureaucracies

A2 yes; productive efficiency means producing with the lowest average costs and says nothing about revenue

A3 by producing more output with the same amount of input

A4 when it is not possible to make anyone better off without making someone else worse off

***examiner's* note** The term 'efficiency' is used in economics in different ways. Productive efficiency occurs when firms use the least number of resources to produce any given level of output. Allocative efficiency takes place when the price of a product is equal to the marginal cost of its production. Dynamic efficiency looks at changing levels of efficiency over time.

 ANSWERS

Capitalism

Q1 What is meant by 'the invisible hand of capitalism'?

Q2 Explain the concept of consumer sovereignty.

Q3 Which of the productive factors — land, labour and capital — cannot be owned? Explain.

Q4 Under capitalism, minimal government is concerned with creating a framework of rules that protects f.......... of c.......... and p.......... p.......... r...........

ANSWERS

an economic system based on private control of production, distribution and exchange

A1 the unseen market forces of supply and demand

A2 when consumer reaction to changes in products and their prices dictates the action of competing producers

A3 labour; since slavery was abolished, it is not possible for one person to own another person

A4 *freedom of contract; private property rights*

***examiner's* note** Under capitalism, most products are allocated through markets by the price mechanism, but there is a minimal role for government where markets fail or are judged imperfect by some efficiency criteria. The action of government needs to be critically evaluated, however, as history offers many examples of government intervention failing to improve upon the situation and arguably making things worse.

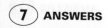 **ANSWERS**

Positive economics

Q1 In contrast to positive statements made by economists, politicians often make n_____ statements about the economy.

Q2 Is it a positive statement to suggest that markets should be made more responsive to price signals? Explain your answer.

Q3 The individual, the firm and the industry are studied in a branch of economics known as m_____.

Q4 What is the main difference between a physical science and a social science?

 ANSWERS

a scientific approach to economics,
involving the collection of facts and
the development of theories

A1 *normative* — also called value judgements

A2 no; the use of the word 'should' implies a value judgement

A3 *microeconomics*; this studies at a small scale, while macroeconomics looks at the national and international economy

A4 in the 'laboratory' of a social science it is not possible to repeat experiments under controlled conditions

***examiner's* note** Value judgements have a part to play in economics, as decisions have to be made, often by politicians under the guidance of economists, about the way the economy is managed. There is a grey area where it is difficult to determine whether a statement is positive or normative, although a rough rule of thumb is that sentences that are positive often include 'was', 'is' or 'will be', while normative sentences include 'should', 'ought', 'could' or 'must'.

Value judgement

Q1 Are value judgements likely to be more necessary in analysis or evaluation?

Q2 'During its term of office, the government needs to ensure a high level of employment.' Is this a positive statement?

Q3 'Over the next 5 years, the rate of inflation is likely to move into line with the Eurozone rate.' Is this a positive statement?

Q4 It is a value judgement that scarce resources are not f............... d...............

ANSWERS

an opinion based upon a belief rather than factual evidence — a normative statement

A1 evaluation; this is often opinion based upon a balanced view of imperfect information

A2 no, it is a value judgement as it is based upon someone's unsubstantiated opinion

A3 yes, because it is based upon the future probability of an event

A4 *fairly distributed*; arguably, resources are not fairly distributed in a free market economy

***examiner's* note** It is sometimes difficult to decide whether a statement is a value judgement or a positive statement based on evidence. It is, however, possible to have an opinion that is not a value judgement but is based upon factual evidence. If economic decisions are based upon perfect knowledge, there is little room for value judgements. However, if knowledge is imperfect, there is greater need to involve value judgements in decision making.

9 **ANSWERS**

Equity

Q1 Does a capitalist system based on markets create equity?

Q2 Does equity fit closer to a positive or a normative analysis?

Q3 Does economics create the equivalent of a political democracy?

Q4 Markets are often criticised for producing a lack of f............... in resource allocation.

ANSWERS

fairness in the way resources are allocated among people

A1 most economists say no, as it creates significant inequalities of income and wealth

A2 normative; what is equitable is often a matter of judgement and therefore fits closer to normative analysis

A3 no; in a political democracy there is one person, one vote, while units of currency create more economic votes for rich people

A4 *fairness*

***examiner's* note** Equity is an area of significant debate in economics. For example:

- Is it fair that a person receives a higher income for working harder than someone else?
- Is it fair that one person's investments increase in value while another's fall?
- Is it fair that an older person has more wealth than a younger person?
- Is it fair that one person inherits an income for life?

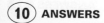 **ANSWERS**

Economic data

Q1 Describe the trends in the following data: 2, 4, 6, 12, 24, 48, 60.

Q2 Total sales of a product are 870,000, 120,000 of which are sold in the Midlands. What percentage of sales occurs in the Midlands?

Q3 Over a 5-year period, the price of a product rose from £1.70 to £4.30. What was the percentage change in price?

Q4 During a 3-year period, yearly price rises were 2.9%, 1.9% and 4.2%. What was the average rate of change per annum?

ANSWERS

A1 the data start with an arithmetic progression, that is, a constant nominal increase; after 6 there is a geometric progression with accelerating nominal growth and constant percentage changes; after 48 the growth rate decelerates

A2 13.8%

A3 152.9%

A4 3%

***examiner's* note** It is important to be able to identify trends and breaks in trend for time-series data. Simple calculations are necessary to support, illustrate and highlight changes. Know the difference between 'a percentage of' and 'a percentage change'. Be aware that the components making up an average may be significantly different from the average. In addition, familiarise yourself with the way index numbers are used and the ways in which data are illustrated using charts, graphs, tables and diagrams.

 **ANSWERS**

Economic forecast

Q1 Is economic forecasting an area of positive or normative economics? Why?

Q2 Are there economic facts about the future? Explain your answer.

Q3 Simple forecasts are often based upon e................. techniques.

Q4 Before a firm changes the price of its product, it is likely to forecast the effect of this upon what?

ANSWERS ▶▶

a prediction about future economic events

A1 positive economics; the likelihood of a future event taking place can be given a probability

A2 no; there are only facts about the past, and all events that have not yet happened can only be forecast with degrees of probability

A3 *extrapolation* — extending past numbers or events into a logical future sequence

A4 sales revenue and profits, not just sales

***examiner's* note** Forecasting is an important branch of economics and arguably the most important task of the professional economist. Economists are employed by private firms, public companies, government departments and international agencies. The UK Treasury uses a complex model of the economy to forecast a whole range of events, which are taken into account by the Chancellor of the Exchequer in preparing the Budget.

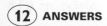

Economic good

Q1 Which two characteristics are used to distinguish a private good from a public good?

Q2 Some private goods are considered to be over-consumed and others under-consumed. What is the name given to each type of product?

Q3 Give an example of an economic good that has the characteristics of both a private good and a public good.

Q4 What is a quasi-public good?

ANSWERS ▶▶

A1 a private good is rival and excludable, while a public good is non-rival and non-excludable

A2 merit goods are under-consumed; demerit goods are over-consumed

A3 inside a theatre, cinema or nightclub, the product has non-rival and non-excludable characteristics, while outside the product is rival and excludable; this product is often referred to as a club good

A4 a product that has all or some of the characteristics of a public good, but which could become a private good if property rights are exercised (e.g. fencing off and limiting access to a sandy beach)

***examiner's* note** The market system is considered to be the most effective way of allocating resources to the supply of private goods. However, some other economic goods are judged to have resources less efficiently allocated to them by the market.

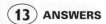

Normal product

Q1 When the price of a product changes, it has both a real i............. and a s............. effect on demand.

Q2 What is the difference between a normal product and an inferior product?

Q3 A Giffen good is an inferior good with a difference. Explain.

Q4 Explain how a bicycle can be a normal good to one person and an inferior good to another.

ANSWERS ▶▶

A1 *income; substitution*

A2 a normal good has a positive relationship to changes in income, while an inferior good has a negative relationship

A3 inferior goods may have normal or perverse demand curves, while all Giffen goods have perverse demand curves

A4 one person may be riding a bicycle because he/she cannot afford a car, while the other may be cycling to keep fit

***examiner's* note** Even though people's nominal income is unaffected by a price change, their real income changes in as much as they can now spend more or less of their income to buy the product. Different segments of a market may have a different response to a change in price. The high-income sector of the economy may consider a product as inferior, whereas the same product may be normal to the low-income sector.

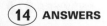

Factors of production

Q1 In economics, the sea is land. Explain.

Q2 What is the dependency ratio?

Q3 Distinguish between capital and wealth.

Q4 What is an entrepreneur?

ANSWERS ▶▶

elements necessary for economic production, usually comprising land, labour, capital and enterprise

A1 the productive factor 'land' includes all natural resources that have an economic use; the sea contains fish and can be used for wave power

A2 the ratio of those who are working to produce goods and services to those who are not working

A3 wealth is what you own at a particular point in time; capital is that part of your wealth that is used to derive a flow of income

A4 a risk taker who combines productive factors to create a product that has no guaranteed rate of return

***examiner's* note** Some textbooks identify only three factors of production: land, which is all the free gifts of nature; capital, which is the produced means of production; and labour, which includes all of the physical and mental effort used in the production of goods and services. In this case, enterprise is considered to be a subset of labour.

 **ANSWERS**

Specialisation and the division of labour

Q1 Which economist in which book pointed out that making pins required 18 distinct operations?

Q2 Identify four advantages of specialising the function of labour.

Q3 What is the relationship between input, output and the division of labour?

Q4 Name two disadvantages of the division of labour.

ANSWERS

A1 Adam Smith in his seminal book *The Wealth of Nations*

A2
- time saving
- increased dexterity
- increased efficiency
- comparative advantage

A3 the same input will produce more output after the division of labour

A4
- monotony
- demotivation

examiner's note Despite the advantages, it is recognised that the repetitive nature of some jobs can demotivate and alienate the workforce. Therefore, in order to enrich the working environment, many companies have tried to develop machines to do repetitive jobs and thereby create a more varied and interesting environment for their workers.

Economies of scale

Q1 If the dimensions of a container are doubled, by how much is the carrying capacity (volume) increased?

Q2 Explain and give an example of an external economy of scale.

Q3 A firm can grow too large and be affected by diseconomies of scale. Give one example of an internal diseconomy of scale.

Q4 Explain and give an example of an external diseconomy of scale.

ANSWERS ▶▶

a decline in unit costs of production due to an increase in size of a firm

A1 eight times, therefore offering a considerable saving on transport costs

A2 something outside the firm that reduces unit costs, e.g. building roads, setting up training centres

A3 internal diseconomies are usually associated with problems of communication, control, morale etc.

A4 something outside the firm that raises unit costs, e.g. road congestion, the bidding up of factor prices

***examiner's* note** Economies of scale occur in the long run when all factors are variable and therefore the size of the firm is not dependent upon varying the proportions of productive factors employed. Internal economies of scale are usually grouped under technical, marketing, financial and risk bearing, while diseconomies are linked to the problems of managing lots of people. Not all firms can achieve economies of scale, which is why some large industries are made up of many small firms.

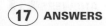

Rational decision

Q1 Given a choice, consumers are assumed to make rational decisions when purchasing products. What does this mean?

Q2 Identify an example of maximising behaviour by entrepreneurs.

Q3 On what assumption is the acceptance that some goods are inferior based?

Q4 What is the rational relationship between a normal good and a change in a person's income?

ANSWERS

an economic decision that is guided by experience

A1 choosing the product that gives the consumer the greatest usefulness per unit of money spent

A2 acting to maximise returns, probably in the form of profits

A3 there must be superior alternatives available

A4 as a person's income increases, he/she will not buy less of a product and will probably buy more

***examiner's* note** Most people will admit to having had a 'rush of blood to the head' when they made a totally irrational purchase. This is usually confirmed when a wardrobe search unearths clothes that have never been worn. This does not invalidate the assumption of rationality behind economic decisions. As long as most people act rationally most of the time, economic models make sense.

Effective demand

Q1 Which two variables are usually negatively related in the concept of demand?

Q2 Explain what is meant by the statement that demand is a time-based relationship.

Q3 What is the importance of 'ceteris paribus' when looking at a demand function?

Q4 Why is it that a person may buy more of a product when the price is reduced?

ANSWERS

when a consumer has both the desire and the ability to purchase a product at a given price

A1 price and quantity are inversely related in a normal demand function

A2 the amount demanded at a certain price is meaningless unless it is related to a week, a month, a year etc.

A3 markets are dynamic places where many variables act and react, and in order to produce a demand function, extraneous variables are held constant, hence the term 'other things being equal'

A4 the usefulness of the product per unit of money spent increases

***examiner's* note** Demand is one of the most important concepts in economics and it is necessary to understand its intricacies, along with its relationship to other important concepts. Remember that in the demand function the independent variable is price and the dependent variable is quantity, i.e. price changes quantity.

Market demand

Q1 What is meant by the statement that market demand is a horizontal sum concept?

Q2 Other than price, identify three variables that can affect market demand.

Q3 Changes in price cause changes in demand and this is illustrated by a m_____ along a demand curve.

Q4 Is a demand curve a realistic concept? Explain your answer.

the sum of all consumers' demand for a product at various prices

A1 the quantity demanded by all consumers at each price is measured on the horizontal axis

A2 possible answers are: income, taste, preferences, relative prices, availability of credit

A3 *movement* (not to be confused with a shift)

A4 no; because ceteris paribus is applied to other variables

***examiner's* note** A normal market demand curve is downward sloping, from left to right, meaning that more will be demanded at lower prices and less at higher prices. However, there are exceptions to the norm, as in the case of Giffen, conspicuous consumption and speculative goods. Here, the demand curve is upward sloping, from left to right, meaning that more is demanded at higher prices and vice versa.

Demand curve shift

Q1 What is the difference between a shift and a movement in demand analysis?

Q2 Explain how a change in relative prices can cause both a movement and a shift of demand curves.

Q3 How may a rise in the price of money shift the demand for cars?

Q4 What will happen to the demand for a particular Panasonic television if Sony raises the price of a similar television?

ANSWERS

when more or less of a product is demanded at the same price

A1 a movement requires a change in price; a shift occurs at the same price

A2 if the price of one product changes, this will cause a movement along its demand curve; the demand for a related product may change and this will be a shift

A3 a rise in interest rates will shift the demand curve for cars to the left, as many cars are purchased on credit

A4 if Sony raises its price, the demand curve for the Panasonic television will shift outwards (to the right)

examiner's note Short-answer questions often require the student to distinguish clearly between shifts and movements in both supply and demand curves. Examiners consider questions in this area to be important in identifying those students who understand economic theory.

 21 ANSWERS

Shifting demand curves

Start at E and say whether the
following will shift the demand curve:

Q1 A real rise in national income.

Q2 A fall in the price of a substitute
good.

Q3 A rise in price.

Q4 A change in tastes.

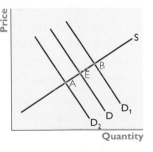

A1 this will shift demand from D to D_1 and produce a new equilibrium at B

A2 this will shift demand from D to D_2 and produce a new equilibrium at A, as less of the product will be demanded at the same price

A3 given no other information, this can only refer to a movement along a demand curve, not a shift

A4 this could shift the demand either way and produce equilibrium at B or A, depending upon whether the change was towards or away from this product

***examiner's* note** A very common mistake is to write that a change in price will change demand and that this is a shift in the demand curve. As a shift is more or less demanded at each and every price, a shift in the demand curve will cause a movement along the supply curve in order to establish a new equilibrium. In addition, note that a change in the price of other products can cause a shift in the demand curve for the product in question.

Price elasticity of demand

Q1 What is the formula for calculating price elasticity of demand?

Q2 Explain the changes on each axis when a demand curve is represented by a rectangular hyperbola.

Q3 How will a business raise more revenue if the product price is on the inelastic part of the demand curve?

Q4 What is the most likely reason for a government to increase the indirect tax on cigarettes?

ANSWERS

a measure of the responsiveness of demand to a change in price

A1 $\dfrac{\text{price elasticity}}{\text{of demand}} = \dfrac{\text{percentage change in quantity demanded}}{\text{percentage change in price}}$

A2 the change on each axis is in the same proportion

A3 the simplest way is to raise the price of the product and reduce sales

A4 the most likely reason is to raise revenue, although the government might say it is to discourage smoking

***examiner's* note** If it is only necessary to say whether a product has inelastic, elastic or unitary demand, use the revenue method to identify whether revenue increases, decreases or remains the same when price changes. Also note that, although every product has a price elasticity of demand, it is not possible to know in reality whether it is the price change or another variable that has affected demand. This limits the usefulness of the concept.

 ANSWERS

Point price elasticity of demand

Q1 Describe the elasticity of points A, B, C, D and E.

Q2 What happens to price, sales and revenue between B and C?

Q3 What happens to price, sales and revenue between C and D?

Q4 What shape is a demand curve with uniform unitary elasticity?

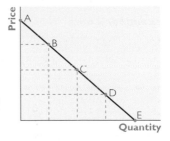

ANSWERS ❯❯

A1 A = infinity, B = elastic, C = unitary, D = inelastic, E = 0

A2 price falls, sales rise, revenue rises

A3 price falls, sales rise, revenue falls

A4 a rectangular hyperbola

***examiner's* note** The diagram on the other side of this card has points of
elasticity that can be measured with a ruler or calculated using percentage
change or average formulae. Measurement using a ruler takes the distance from
the point in question along the curve to the horizontal axis and divides by the
distance to the vertical axis:
- Point C is equidistant between the axes and CE/CA = 1
- Point A = AE/A = infinity
- Point B = BE/BA and is elastic
- Point D is DE/DA and is inelastic
- Point E is E/EA = 0

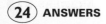 **ANSWERS**

Cross elasticity of demand

Q1 What is the formula for calculating cross elasticity of demand?

Q2 A negative cross elasticity of demand is a n............ but not s............ condition for products to be c............ .

Q3 The cross elasticity of demand for two products is 0.75. What effect did a price change of 5% for one product have on the demand for the other product?

Q4 What is the relationship between the two products described in Q3? Give an example.

ANSWERS

a measure of the responsiveness of demand for one product to a change in the price of another

A1 $\dfrac{\text{cross elasticity}}{\text{of demand}} = \dfrac{\text{percentage change in quantity demanded of X}}{\text{percentage change in the price of Y}}$

A2 *necessary; sufficient; complementary*

A3 $0.75 = \dfrac{x}{5} \therefore x = 3.75$ (a change of 3.75% in quantity demanded)

A4 the products are likely to be substitutes as the cross elasticity of demand is positive, e.g. gas or electricity, pork or beef

***examiner's* note** Cross elasticity of demand calculations that are zero or infinity relate to products that are independent of each other. However, as Q2 suggests, it may be that two products show a positive or negative cross elasticity of demand but are only related in the calculation by chance — hence the reference to *necessary but not sufficient*. To help your revision, note that all elasticity calculations have quantity as the numerator and price or income as the denominator.

(25) **ANSWERS**

Income elasticity of demand

Q1 What is the formula for calculating income elasticity of demand?

Q2 What is the difference between the income elasticity of demand of a normal product and that of an inferior product?

Q3 Income elasticity of demand = 1.2. The percentage change in income is 5%. What is the percentage change in quantity demanded?

Q4 Is the product identified in Q3 likely to be a luxury or a necessity?

ANSWERS

a measure of the responsiveness of demand to a change in income

A1 $\dfrac{\text{income elasticity}}{\text{of demand}} = \dfrac{\text{percentage change in quantity demanded}}{\text{percentage change in income}}$

A2   the income elasticity of demand of a normal product is always positive, while an inferior product has a negative value

A3 $1.2 = \dfrac{x}{5} \therefore x = 6$ (demand increases by 6%)

A4   the income elasticity of demand of a necessity is less than 1 or inelastic, therefore the product in question is likely to be a luxury

examiner's note The Engel curve plots the relationship between a change in income measured on the horizontal axis and a change in consumer demand measured on the vertical axis. The slope of the curve is positive for normal products and negative for inferior products and, as a ratio of a change in consumption to a change in income, it illustrates the marginal propensity to consume.

Income elasticity of demand for different products

Describe a product that may have
the characteristics illustrated
between:

 O and A

 A and B

 B and C

 C and D

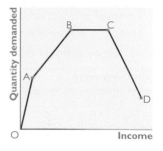

ANSWERS

A1 a normal product with income-elastic demand (a luxury)

A2 a normal product with income-inelastic demand (an essential product)

A3 a normal product with zero income elasticity that may already have been consumed up to the maximum required

A4 an inferior product that has a superior alternative

examiner's **note** One product could have all the characteristics described in the diagram during its life cycle. For example, a colour television could have been a luxury that turned into an essential product as income increased. At some point, the television could even become an inferior good as home cinema systems become the choice of high-income earners.

Derived demand

Q1 Distinguish between final demand and derived demand.

Q2 Name two things in derived demand when a person consumes a pint of beer.

Q3 What is the effect on products in derived demand when the producer raises the price of the product to the consumer?

Q4 Which of the following is in derived demand: (a) a taxi; (b) crude oil; (c) a cricket bat?

ANSWERS

where demand for productive factors and components is determined by product demand

A1   a product in final demand is for consumption, while a product in derived demand is for production

A2   any of the ingredients of beer (i.e. water, yeast, hops) or the productive factors (labour, capital, enterprise)

A3   if the product price is raised, demand will fall and the demand curves for components and productive factors will shift to the left

A4   all are in derived demand because they are used to produce something else, i.e. a taxi ride, petroleum and batting

***examiner's* note** Consumers do not gain any satisfaction from products or productive factors in derived demand. Only when consumers use the product in final demand do they gain satisfaction. The independent variable in this relationship is demand, while the product or productive factor in derived demand is a dependent variable.

Market supply

Q1 What is the normal shape for a market supply curve?

Q2 Other than price, identify two factors that may affect market supply.

Q3 How does the market place deal with an excess supply of a product?

Q4 Why do house prices usually rise by more than the rate of inflation, while computer prices rise by less?

ANSWERS

the sum of all the firms' output at different prices for a particular product

A1 upward sloping from left to right, as it is profitable to produce more at higher prices

A2 changes in productivity; changes in factor prices

A3 there may be sale prices to clear the surplus

A4 the supply of land is restricted and so is the supply of houses, whereas it is much easier to expand the supply of computers and reduce production costs

***examiner's* note** The market supply curve is the horizontal sum of all the individual firms' supply curves. Although it is usually upward sloping from left to right, there are special cases:

• it is horizontal or perfectly elastic when marginal costs are constant
• it is downward sloping from left to right in the case of the supply of currency to a foreign exchange market, when the demand for imports is inelastic

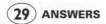

(29) ANSWERS

Supply curve shift

Q1 Is a shift in a supply curve vertical or horizontal?

Q2 In which direction does the curve shift when government imposes (a) an indirect tax, (b) a subsidy on a product?

Q3 Which factor is most likely to cause a shift in the supply curve for a cereal farmer?

Q4 Give an example of two goods in joint supply and say what will happen to the supply curve of one product if there is a movement along the other supply curve.

ANSWERS

A1 both — the vertical shift means the same amount is supplied at a different price, while the horizontal shift means more or less is supplied at the same price

A2 (a) shifts to the left; (b) shifts to the right

A3 a change in the weather

A4 Examples include beef and hide, lead and zinc; a movement along one curve causes a shift in the other

***examiner's* note** A shift in supply occurs when more or less is supplied at the same price, while a movement occurs when more or less is supplied at different prices. Shifts are often associated with changes in the cost of production. Changes in factor prices or technology cause the profit-maximising entrepreneur to increase or decrease output at a given price to equate marginal revenue with marginal cost.

Shifting supply curves

Start at E and say whether the
following will shift the supply curve:

Q1 Strike action.

Q2 Increased call charges.

Q3 Good harvests.

Q4 A product becoming
fashionable.

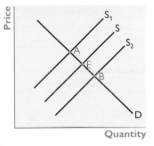

ANSWERS ▶▶

A1 this will reduce supply at each and every price and shift S to S_1, producing a new equilibrium at A

A2 this will increase production costs and shift S to S_1, producing a new equilibrium at A

A3 more will be supplied at each and every price and supply will shift from S to S_2, producing a new equilibrium at B

A4 this will shift the demand curve, not the supply curve

examiner's note There are two main reasons why supply curves shift. Firstly, a change in the costs of production changes the equilibrium position for a profit-maximising producer. A rise in marginal cost means that, under normal circumstances, it will equate with marginal revenue at a lower level of output. Alternatively, a fall in marginal cost means it will equate with marginal revenue at a higher level of output. Secondly, there can be an inadvertent increase or decrease in the supply of a product, as often happens in the agricultural industry.

Supply curves

Q1 Which two curves have the same elasticity?

Q2 Which curve best fits a situation of high unemployment?

Q3 A firm runs out of stocks. Which curve best fits the short run?

Q4 A price rise has no effect on supply. What is the elasticity?

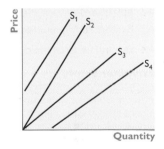

ANSWERS

A1 S_2 and S_3; both are unitary, as they are straight lines that pass through the origin

A2 S_4; when unemployment is high, it is easier to employ additional productive factors and the supply curve is elastic — the most elastic supply curve is S_4

A3 S_1; the supply curve becomes more inelastic

A4 the curve is perfectly inelastic with a zero price elasticity of supply

***examiner's* note** The price elasticity of supply depends upon the ease with which a firm or firms can or cannot expand and contract output. Time is an important factor. For example, firms may have agreements with unions that they cannot change working practices without 24 hours' notice and therefore output is perfectly inelastic for at least a day. Moreover, time and elasticity of supply are not constants across industries, as some may be able to make a full adjustment to price changes in a few days, while other industries may take a few years.

Price elasticity of supply

Q1 What is the formula for calculating price elasticity of supply?

Q2 Any straight-line supply curve that would pass through the origin of a price and quantity graph has a u............... elasticity.

Q3 What effect is the momentary period, the short run and the long run likely to have on supply elasticity?

Q4 What is meant by the statement, 'supply elasticity is influenced in the short run by the excess capacity in a firm'?

ANSWERS

a measure of the responsiveness of the quantity supplied to a change in the price of the product

A1 $\text{price elasticity of supply} = \dfrac{\text{percentage change in quantity supplied}}{\text{percentage change in price}}$

A2 *unitary*

A3 supply will be perfectly inelastic in the momentary period and is likely to be inelastic in the short run and more elastic in the long run

A4 if a firm has excess capacity, the short-run supply curve will be more elastic

***examiner's* note** In the same way that any straight line passing through the origin has unitary elasticity, any straight line that would cut the horizontal axis has an inelastic value between 0 and 1, while any straight line that would cut the vertical axis has an elastic value between 1 and infinity. This always applies, no matter how steep or shallow the lines may appear.

Equilibrium

Q1 What is a marketplace?

Q2 Is the internet a marketplace? Explain.

Q3 What is an equilibrium price?

Q4 Explain how a shift and a movement are connected in a dynamic market.

ANSWERS ▶▶

a position of balance that will not change unless one of its component variables changes

A1 where buyers and sellers of products meet in order to complete a trade

A2 yes; buyers and sellers conduct deals on a worldwide scale

A3 a price that produces a position of balance (or equality) between producers and consumers of a product

A4 in a changing market, a shift in either a supply or a demand curve will cause a movement along the other curve

***examiner's* note** A simple market produces an equality where the demand curve intersects the supply curve. However, because it is recognised that markets are forever changing, it is unlikely that a market with its many variables will ever be in a static equilibrium. The best that can be expected is that dynamic markets will tend towards equilibrium as prices are set to clear markets and avoid surpluses or shortages.

Market equilibrium

Which area represents:

Q1 Consumer surplus?

Q2 Producer surplus?

Q3 A measure of maximum efficiency?

Q4 The revenue received by producers?

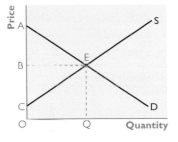

ANSWERS ▶▶

A1 ABE (the area enclosed by the price line BE and the demand curve AE)

A2 BEC (the part of the revenue received by producers that is surplus to the minimum required to produce that amount)

A3 ACE (maximised when resources are considered to be used efficiently)

A4 OBEQ (the area represented by price × quantity)

examiner's note The static equilibrium market diagram is an important model to learn, draw and label correctly. The two functions represented by the demand curve and the supply curve need to be understood. Their manipulation and the areas they represent provide a simple, basic model upon which much more complex ideas, theories and hypotheses can be developed.

Consumer surplus

Q1 If the market price of a product is £7 and a consumer is prepared to pay £10 for the first unit, £9 for the second, £8 for the third and £7 for the fourth, what is the surplus?

Q2 Is consumer surplus the triangle above or below the price line?

Q3 What shape for a demand curve eliminates consumer surplus?

Q4 It is possible to eliminate consumer surplus if a producer can pursue p............ d.............

ANSWERS ▶▶

the difference between the maximum
a consumer is willing to pay for
a product and the amount paid

A1 $(10 + 9 + 8 + 7) - (7 \times 4) = £6$

A2 it is the triangle above the price line, where the demand curve
illustrates the higher prices that consumers are prepared to pay

A3 a perfectly elastic demand curve eliminates the gap between the
demand curve and the price line

A4 *price discrimination* — this eliminates the consumer surplus by
charging each consumer the maximum price he/she is prepared
to pay

examiner's **note** Price discrimination can take place only if it is possible to
segment a market and stop any resale between parts of the market. It is also
necessary to have monopoly control over the supply of the product. An example
is a distinguished surgeon who could charge different prices to the rich and poor
without any fear that they could resell the operation.

Producer surplus

Q1 If a producer is prepared to offer 1 unit for sale at a price of £6, 2 units at £7, 3 units at £8, 4 units at £9 and 5 units at £10, what is the producer surplus at a market price of £10?

Q2 Why are producers prepared to supply more of a product as the market price rises?

Q3 Under normal circumstances, will a rightward shift in the demand curve increase or decrease producer surplus? Why?

Q4 How does efficiency relate to producer and consumer surplus?

ANSWERS

revenue received by the producer
above that which would have brought
the product on to the market

A1 $10 \times 5 - (10 + 9 + 8 + 7 + 6) = £10$

A2 their total profits will increase

A3 increase; the area below the price line and above the supply
curve increases

A4 an efficient allocation of resources will maximise the combined
area of producer and consumer surplus

examiner's note In theory, a producer will stop producing when the
additional cost of producing one more product is equal to the additional revenue
received from selling that product. When the market price rises, the additional
revenue received rises and allows the producer to expand, even when the
additional cost of production is rising. In reality, it is difficult to be so precise and
all that can be said is that the producer will tend towards this position.

Market disequilibrium

Q1 What happens in the market if the price is P_1?

Q2 What happens if the government fixes the price at P_1?

Q3 What happens if a maximum pricing policy sets the price at P_3?

Q4 What happens if a minimum pricing policy sets the price at P_3?

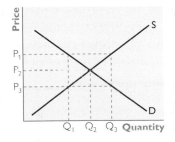

A1 the market is in disequilibrium and forces will act to reduce the market surplus as price falls from P_1 to P_2 and quantity falls from Q_3 to Q_2

A2 a persistent surplus of $Q_3 - Q_1$ will be unsold in the market

A3 Q_3 will be demanded by consumers and Q_1 will be supplied by producers, leading to a persistent shortage

A4 the market-clearing equilibrium P_2Q_2 will prevail, as there is no incentive for market forces to push prices any lower

***examiner's* note** Candidates often make a mistake when explaining what will happen if a maximum or minimum price is set either side of the market-clearing price. Both pricing policies allow the price to adjust one way but not the other. Therefore, if a maximum price is set below, or a minimum price above, market price, then a shortage or surplus occurs. In contrast, the market price prevails if the maximum is set above or the minimum below.

Disequilibrium

Q1 What are the assumptions upon which the actions of a producer and a consumer are founded?

Q2 If a market price is above the equilibrium price, what will happen in the market?

Q3 When a price changes, are producers or consumers likely to react more quickly?

Q4 If a market price is below the equilibrium price, what will happen in the market?

ANSWERS

an imbalance between supply and demand in a market, requiring adjustments to price and/or quantity

A1 producers are assumed to maximise profit while consumers aim to maximise satisfaction

A2 an excess supply will cause producers to lower price and contract output

A3 consumers react more quickly as the time lag for producers is constrained by the need to change the use of productive factors

A4 excess demand will cause producers to raise price and expand output

***examiner's* note** Based upon the desire a consumer has for value for money and the producer has for profits, market forces will be set in motion as soon as a disequilibrium occurs. These forces act to the benefit of both producers and consumers and are the 'invisible hand' mentioned by Adam Smith. They allocate resources without the administration costs and bureaucracy that exist in a command economy.

 **ANSWERS**

Cobweb theory

Q1 Why is it unlikely that stable prices will exist in a market for agricultural crops?

Q2 What is likely to be the biggest influence on this year's crop sowing?

Q3 Why might farmers be happier with bad harvests than with good harvests?

Q4 What policy is used in the EU to stabilise prices and what is its most likely effect on output?

ANSWERS

a theory of price that recognises an unpredictable supply and a time lag between decision and execution

A1 variable supply and degrees of perishability cause prices to rise and fall

A2 last year's prices for various crops will influence plans for this year's crops

A3 bad harvests force prices up and increase profit margins, while good harvests depress prices and increase the likelihood of bankruptcy

A4 minimum price guarantees; they may be fixed too high and cause over-supply

***examiner's* note** The cobweb theory is so named because a tracing of price and output for successive years gradually moves towards the intersection of supply and demand curves and gives the visual appearance of a cobweb. If the supply elasticity is less than the demand elasticity, a stable cobweb with a tendency to move towards equilibrium will exist. An elasticity of supply that is greater than the demand elasticity tends to produce an unstable cobweb moving away from the equilibrium.

 **ANSWERS**

Market failure

Q1 What is a collective consumption good?

Q2 What is street lighting an example of?

Q3 Is it necessary for government to finance the production and consumption of a public good in order to create a marketplace?

Q4 For which of the following products does the market fail: drugs, law and order, education?

ANSWERS

inability of the marketplace to allocate resources to the production of certain useful products

A1 a product that consumers want, but are not prepared to buy as they cannot exclude other consumers from using it

A2 a public good, also referred to as a collective consumption good

A3 it is only necessary to finance the consumption of a public good to produce a marketplace

A4 law and order; this is not consumed by individuals whereas education and drugs are

examiner's **note** Some textbooks assume that public goods that are non-rival and non-excludable need to be both produced and consumed under the direction of a third party, usually government. However, it is possible for the marketplace to supply these products as long as the third party finances the demand. In fact, there is almost total agreement among economists that taxation should be used to finance the demand for a public good, as without it the market would totally fail.

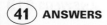
41 ANSWERS

Market imperfection

Q1 Explain how the distribution of knowledge creates a market imperfection.

Q2 Identify a reason why the pharmaceutical industry is imperfect.

Q3 Does advertising increase or reduce market imperfection?

Q4 What characteristic of power generation is likely to create an imperfect market?

ANSWERS

when there is an inefficient allocation of resources in product and productive factor markets

A1 only if knowledge is perfect will it produce an efficient allocation of information

A2 patents are an effective barrier to competition

A3 arguably informative advertising may reduce imperfection while persuasive advertising may increase imperfection

A4 technical economies of scale lead to the existence of oligopolistic firms

***examiner's* note** Given imperfection, markets can still allocate resources, albeit with degrees of inefficiency. In some textbooks, market imperfections are separated from market failure, where the market does not even partially allocate resources. In other textbooks, market failure is considered to be an extreme form of market imperfection. The two main factors creating imperfections are imperfect information and market dominance by large firms.

Public good

Q1 When is an army not a public good?

Q2 What is meant by non-rival?

Q3 What is meant by non-excludable?

Q4 An area of economics concerned with applying economic principles to the political decision-making process in the non-market sector is called the theory of p............ c............

ANSWERS

product with collective demand, non-excludable and non-rival characteristics, not produced in a market

A1 rich people may hire their own private army to protect them and/or their property

A2 if a firm produces a public good, it cannot limit who consumes it

A3 when offered to any one person, a non-excludable good also becomes available to all other people

A4 *public choice*; among other things, public choice theory looks at public goods and collective consumption

***examiner's* note** Theoretically, public goods are at the other extreme from private goods, which are totally rival and excludable. However, in reality it is difficult to find products that fit the extreme model. For example, street lighting is often used as an example, but by its very location a street light favours some people more than others. A second often-quoted example is the police, who may provide a public service but also provide a private service when, for example, they are on duty at a football ground.

Excludable/non-excludable

Q1 Which of the following products are excludable or non-excludable: a lighthouse, housing, the Royal Navy, HM Customs?

Q2 What is the difference between excludable and non-excludable?

Q3 Is the satellite signal for Sky television excludable or non-excludable?

Q4 Is a family doctor who works for the NHS providing an excludable or non-excludable service?

ANSWERS

offered to individual consumers, a product is excludable; offered to all, it is non-excludable

A1 the Royal Navy, HM Customs and the lighthouse are non-excludable; housing can be provided separately to individuals and is excludable

A2 excludable products can be provided to some consumers and not others, while non-excludable products are available to everyone

A3 it is a non-excludable signal that can be made excludable by encryption

A4 an excludable service, as the service provided is limited to the user

***examiner's* note** There is often confusion over the precise difference between rival/excludable and non-rival/non-excludable. The easiest way to avoid this is to recognise that excludable and non-excludable characterise the provision of the good or service by the producer, while rival and non-rival characterise the consumption of the product by the consumer. Note that it is possible for a product to have mixed characteristics as in the case of Sky television, where the signal is non-excludable but the product is made marketable by encryption.

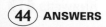

Rival/non-rival

Q1 Is a theatrical production rival or non-rival?

Q2 Is the reception of BBC television rival or non-rival?

Q3 Why is being rival an essential characteristic for the provision of a private good?

Q4 Are rival products diminishable?

ANSWERS ▶▶

if, by using a product, a consumer restricts its consumption, it is rival; if not, it is non-rival

A1 it has both characteristics; the performance is non-rival to members of the audience, but rival to anyone else

A2 non-rival; its consumption by one person does not restrict its consumption by other people

A3 consumers will not pay for products if they cannot restrict their use to themselves

A4 yes; in some textbooks diminishable and non-diminishable are synonymous with rival and non-rival

***examiner's* note** The price mechanism can work to allocate resources only if products have rival characteristics. No one will part with money to consume a product if they cannot stop other people from consuming it or if they could have consumed it as a free rider. This situation should not be confused with one where a product is rival when consumed but provides positive externalities that benefit third parties.

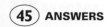

45 ANSWERS

Quasi-public good

Q1 What is a free rider?

Q2 Is a national park a public good?

Q3 Is a good surfing beach a private good?

Q4 In reality, it is very difficult to identify whether some economic products are p............... or p................

ANSWERS ▶▶

product with some or all characteristics of a public good, but can become private if conditions change

A1 an individual who attempts to gain the benefits from a product that has been purchased by someone else

A2 a national park may be a natural asset available to everyone or access may be limited if entry can be controlled, making it a quasi-public good or a private good

A3 it could be if entry to the beach can be controlled and it also has diminishable characteristics, particularly if it becomes overcrowded

A4 *private*; *public*; the changing nature of products makes it difficult to determine whether they are pure private or pure public goods

***examiner's* note** Gifts of nature may start with the characteristics of a public good, but as they grow more popular and if property rights are exercised, they may become private goods.

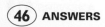

Merit good

Q1 Give two examples of merit goods.

Q2 Why is a merit good likely to be under-consumed?

Q3 Is a merit good a type of public good or private good?

Q4 If a merit good is provided free to the consumer, does it have an opportunity cost?

ANSWERS

product with rival and excludable characteristics that has external benefits and may be under-consumed

A1 education and health are the most quoted examples

A2 current consumers may not have full information about the current and future benefits

A3 private good; it has rival and excludable characteristics

A4 yes; it has an opportunity cost of production even though it does not have an opportunity cost of consumption

examiner's **note** In the case of education and health, there is information failure regarding potential benefits from consuming these products. The balance between private and external benefits also varies considerably across the range of products offered. For example, a surgical procedure has almost entirely private benefits, while a vaccination against a very rare contagious disease gives rise to predominantly external benefits, because the chance of catching it is lowered as more people are vaccinated.

 **ANSWERS**

Demerit good

Q1 Give two examples of demerit goods.

Q2 Why is a demerit good likely to be over-consumed?

Q3 What type of tax is used to manage consumption of a demerit good?

Q4 What is the likely price elasticity of demand for a demerit good?

ANSWERS

product with rival and excludable characteristics that has external costs and may be over-consumed

A1 tobacco and alcohol are two of the most quoted examples

A2 consumers may not have full information about the potential for damage to themselves and society

A3 an indirect/expenditure tax is used to raise the price of demerit goods and reduce their consumption

A4 demerit goods often have addictive qualities that cause their demand to be relatively inelastic

***examiner's* note** Demerit goods such as alcohol, tobacco and gambling are significant revenue earners for government. Although it may take the moral high ground and suggest that it is taxing these products to reduce demand, government is also very dependent on the revenue. The main factor that has limited tax rises recently on tobacco and alcohol is the opening up of the European market, where taxes are much lower on these products.

Positive externalities

Q1 What are MPB and MSB?

Q2 Give an example of a product with the suggested profile.

Q3 What is a market equilibrium and a socially efficient equilibrium?

Q4 How could government internalise the externality?

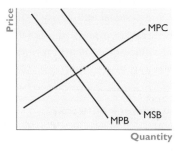

ANSWERS

external benefits from production or consumption that have unpaid spillover effects on a third party

A1 marginal social benefit comprises the marginal private benefits to the individual and the marginal external benefit to society

A2 an example is education, where there are benefits both to the individual and to society

A3 market equilibrium is where MPC intersects MPB; a socially efficient equilibrium output is where MPC intersects MSB

A4 one way to intervene would be to increase output and lower price by imposing a subsidy on the product

examiner's **note** External benefits may be known to exist, but they may require a judgement to estimate their value to society. In the case of education, it has also been difficult to judge whether subsidised education or free education is more beneficial for society. This argument is particularly pertinent to the debate surrounding the way university education should be financed.

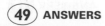 **ANSWERS**

Social benefit

Q1 Which of the following is/are social benefits from purchasing a particular product: consumer satisfaction, third party satisfaction?

Q2 What is a marginal social benefit?

Q3 Which benefit is difficult to value?

Q4 Identify a product that has a relatively high social benefit and a low private benefit.

ANSWERS

the total benefit from a product, to both the private individual and externally to society

A1 both are social benefits; they include benefits to the consumer and to society

A2 the additional benefit to the consumer and to society of consuming one more product

A3 the external benefit to society is difficult to measure, whereas the private benefit can be related to the price paid

A4 among others, education has a social benefit in excess of its private benefit

***examiner's* note** As a group, merit goods have social benefits that are greater than their private benefits. Arguably, railways fit into the same category because the external benefits to society of a person travelling on the train are less pollution in the atmosphere and a lower risk of congestion on the roads. This has led to a debate over the degree of government intervention in the rail network.

 **50** ANSWERS

Negative externalities

Q1 Explain the labels on the curves.

Q2 Where is the external cost on the diagram?

Q3 If the externality is pollution, why do MPC and MSC diverge?

Q4 How could the government intervene to internalise the externality?

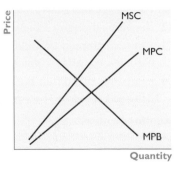

ANSWERS

external costs from either production or consumption that have unpaid spillover effects on a third party

A1 marginal social cost (MSC) is the total cost of production including marginal private costs (MPC) and external costs, while MPB is the marginal private benefit

A2 the vertical distance between MPC and MSC

A3 a certain amount of pollution can be absorbed and recycled naturally, but after a point, the damaging side-effect increases

A4 by placing an indirect tax on the product equal to the value of damage caused by the externality

***examiner's* note** In reality, it is difficult to measure the value of an external cost. It is therefore unlikely that the exact value of a negative externality could be internalised by government action. It should also be noted that there are alternative ways of dealing with external costs such as pollution (e.g. permits, legislation, bans, private property rights).

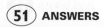

Social cost

Q1 Which of the following is/are social costs: wages, interest, pollution, congestion?

Q2 What is meant by marginal social cost?

Q3 What is the problem of valuing social costs?

Q4 When are social costs equal to the private costs of producing a good or service?

ANSWERS ▶▶

the total cost of production, recognising the private costs to the firm and the external costs to society

A1 they are all social costs; wages and interest are private costs and pollution and congestion are external costs

A2 the additional cost to the firm and to society of producing one more product

A3 the difficulty of putting a value on external costs

A4 when there are no external costs of production

***examiner's* note** It is a common mistake to refer to social costs as external costs and to ignore the fact that social costs refer to the total costs of production. There is a significant economic problem when social costs are much higher than private costs, as this means that society it subsidising the product price and the product is likely to be over-consumed. This may require some government intervention to improve efficiency.

Pollution

Q1 Identify three different types of pollution.

Q2 When is pollution a market imperfection?

Q3 Compared to an efficient market, does pollution produce over-consumption or under-consumption of a product?

Q4 Identify two ways in which the market imperfection of pollution can be alleviated.

ANSWERS

an offending by-product of an economic activity that reduces economic welfare

A1 any offence to the senses, such as loud noises, smells, visual distortion, river pollution and damage to health

A2 when it is an unpaid-for side-effect of production

A3 over-consumption; products are over-consumed because pollution is an external cost to society

A4 answers could include legal controls or bans, indirect taxation and permits to pollute

***examiner's* note** The waste products of economic activity are usually referred to as pollution, although they are only pollution if they have a damaging effect. For example, a factory may dump waste in a local river and it could feed the fish and increase the stock of fish in the river. It should also be recognised that a certain level of pollution can be absorbed and rendered harmless by the actions of nature, so a certain level of pollution is acceptable.

Information failure

Q1 Does advertising help solve the problem of information failure?

Q2 Explain how information failure could lead to inappropriate pricing in the health insurance market.

Q3 What information failure exists in the markets for demerit goods?

Q4 Information failure is more realistic than the assumption in perfect competition that consumers and producers have p............ k.............

ANSWERS

leads to market imperfections and a misallocation of resources

A1 persuasive advertising may create or not improve information failure; informative advertising aims to reduce information failure

A2 consumers of these products have an incentive not to provide all the correct information in order to keep the premium lower

A3 people consuming, for example, cigarettes and alcohol are not convinced of the potential damage such goods can cause in later life

A4 *perfect knowledge*; this is a simplifying but unrealistic assumption of perfect competition

***examiner's* note** In many markets, information failure exists but not at a level that causes a significant misallocation of resources. However, the producer does not always seek to provide total information, and consumers may be persuaded to buy products when they are not fully aware of their usefulness and reliability. Attempts to improve the flow of information and eliminate misrepresentation increase efficiency.

 **ANSWERS**

Black market

Q1 Why might FA Cup Final tickets be priced at P_1?

Q2 Explain the shape of the supply curve.

Q3 Which two factors are likely to produce a black market at the final?

Q4 A black market will reduce some of the c............ s............

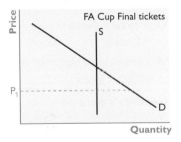

ANSWERS ▶▶

an illegal market that may have developed
after a price has been set below
the market-clearing price

A1 to reward the fans and ensure a full ground

A2 the supply curve is perfectly inelastic at the level of the ground's
capacity

A3 • excess demand
• people with a supply of surplus tickets

A4 *consumer surplus*; this will be reduced as some people will pay
a higher price

***examiner's* note** Often venues where there is a seating capacity will create
the right conditions for setting up a black market. Promoters of sports events
and concerts often set a price slightly below market price in order to ensure
that the venue is full. Other black markets exist when there is demand for a
product that can't be sold legally (e.g. drugs).

 (55) ANSWERS

Government intervention

Q1 For which group of products is there most agreement that governments should intervene?

Q2 If the government provides a good free to the consumer, is it likely to be over- or under-consumed?

Q3 Which type of analysis is usually undertaken before government intervenes?

Q4 For which products is government most likely to use an indirect tax to manage resource allocation?

ANSWERS

action undertaken by a group of people empowered to make decisions on behalf of a country's citizens

A1 there is almost universal agreement that taxes should be used to provide public goods

A2 over-consumed as the usefulness of the product will not need to be considered in respect of its price

A3 cost–benefit analysis is used as a measure of potential efficiency

A4 demerit goods; consumption of these goods can be discouraged by imposing an indirect tax to raise the price

***examiner's* note** There is a significant debate about the extent to which government can intervene in an economy and improve the allocation of resources. Even in the case of public goods, while it is recognised that collective demand requires the government to purchase the product on behalf of society, it is not always thought necessary for government to supply the product. Wherever possible, it seems that private suppliers are being used.

Indirect tax

Q1 Give an example of an *ad valorem* tax.

Q2 What is the difference between a specific tax and an *ad valorem* tax?

Q3 Using the diagram, identify: an increase in VAT; a reduction in an excise duty.

Q4 Is it likely that merit or demerit goods will have an indirect tax placed upon them?

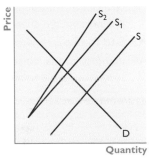

ANSWERS

payment to government levied on specified goods and services, alternatively called an expenditure tax

A1 the obvious example is value added tax

A2 a specific tax is when nominal amounts of money are placed on each unit of output at the point of sale, while an *ad valorem* tax is a percentage change

A3 S to S_2 (a percentage change); S_1 to S (a nominal change)

A4 demerit goods; these will have indirect taxes placed upon them to discourage demand

***examiner's* note** Indirect taxes are expenditure taxes that can be used to deal with certain market imperfections. In the case of a demerit good, the indirect tax can be used to raise price and reduce demand. Cigarettes, alcohol and gambling are examples of demerit goods upon which significant expenditure taxes have been placed. If the tax is specific, the shift in the supply curve is parallel. If it is a percentage, the shifting curve diverges.

 **57 ANSWERS**

Pollution rights

Q1 In economic analysis, can people have a right to pollute?

Q2 What effect will selling rights to pollute have?

Q3 Under what circumstances is it usually illegal to sell a right to pollute?

Q4 Given the sale of pollution permits, how could a local conservationist group reduce pollution?

ANSWERS

A1 yes; if they pay for that right and therefore the externality is internalised

A2 it reduces pollution, as firms have to pay to pollute and some may, therefore, install equipment to stop the pollution

A3 if the pollution in question is likely to damage someone's health or put his/her life at risk

A4 by buying up the pollution rights and not using them to pollute

***examiner's* note** Establishing pollution rights recognises that a certain amount of pollution is acceptable and automatically controls the overall amount. It makes the producer and consumer of the product pay society for the pollution caused. It is argued that pollution permits that control the overall amount of pollution can, without damage to the environment, be resold on a secondary market if they are unused by the original buyer.

Congestion costs

Q1 Identify two examples of the costs of congestion.

Q2 Identify three possible solutions to the problem of congestion.

Q3 Give an example of a town or city that has used economic principles to overcome the problem of congestion.

Q4 Is there a solution to congestion using cars, trains, taxation and subsidy?

ANSWERS

A1 • increased time to complete an activity
   • increased pollution from idling vehicles

A2 • improve alternative routes
   • raise a congestion charge for using the roads
   • increase the cost of travel (e.g. raise tax on petrol)

A3 London is the obvious example, as it is using pricing (congestion charges) to discourage cars

A4 since trains have external benefits, subsidise them and tax cars

***examiner's* note** London has piloted the first congestion charging scheme in the UK, and a measure of its success is the fact that other towns are planning to introduce similar schemes. But there are drawbacks. In London, congestion has increased in those roads just outside the designated area and the local economy has suffered inside the charging zone.

Subsidy

Q1 From P_1Q_1, a subsidy to a firm will produce which equilibrium?

Q2 Why might subsidies be applied to merit goods?

Q3 Give two other reasons for subsidising production.

Q4 What effect does a subsidy have on the demand curve?

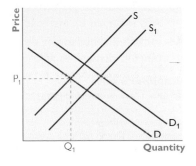

ANSWERS ▶▶

A1 the supply curve will shift right and the new equilibrium will be at the intersection of S_1 and D

A2 to increase the consumption of a product with external benefits

A3 • to lower the price of essential products
  • to maintain or increase employment in vulnerable industries

A4 it causes a movement down (not a shift in) the demand curve as more is demanded at a lower price

***examiner's* note** Subsidies are often used for political rather than economic reasons. For example, using subsidies to maintain employment in a loss-making industry is likely to lead to an inefficient allocation of resources. In the past, subsidies have been placed on essential goods like bread and milk to keep their price down. This is likely to distort the market and does not target low-income groups as the subsidised product is available to all.

Progressive taxation

Q1 Identify a commonly used redistributive tax.

Q2 What is the difference between progressive and regressive taxation?

Q3 As income rises, do people pay more or less tax if the tax is regressive?

Q4 Does progressive income tax redistribute income or wealth or both?

ANSWERS ▸▸

when the marginal rate of tax is higher than the average rate of tax

A1 income tax is the most commonly used redistributive tax

A2 under a progressive tax as income rises a greater proportion of the income is paid in tax, while under a regressive system a smaller proportion is paid

A3 they may pay more tax, but it is always a proportionally smaller amount of their rising incomes

A4 it redistributes income and reduces the ability to accumulate wealth

examiner's note There is a debate about whether progressive tax is the best way of dealing with the perceived market failure of an unequal distribution of income. In the past, income tax has been raised to such a point that it may have discouraged the earning of marginal income, encouraged tax evasion and avoidance, and encouraged emigration of high income earners.

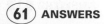

when intervention to correct
market failure does not improve,
or reduces, economic efficiency

A1 yes, but it is difficult to do this precisely because of the need to use estimates and value judgements

A2 not necessarily; there may still be an excess of total benefits over costs when externalities are included

A3 possible answers are taxation, borrowing and sales revenue

A4 *choice; quality; motivate*

***examiner's* note** Naively, in the past, government actions were thought to take place at no cost and always to the benefit of society. Arguably, governments become involved in trying to correct market failure for political reasons and it is now recognised that they do not always have the information or expertise to improve the situation. Some economists have argued that it is rare for governments to improve upon market mechanisms and it is recognised that markets do not include administrative and bureaucratic costs in the allocative process.

Income transfers

Q1 Identify two types of income transfer used by government to deal with inequality.

Q2 What is the umbrella term for cash transfers such as income support and Jobseeker's Allowance?

Q3 What is specific about housing benefits as opposed to other benefits such as the state pension?

Q4 Explain the difference between income transfers and in-kind transfers.

used by government as a means of redistributing income in pursuit of social policy

A1 • transfer from people in work to those out of work
   • transfer from rich to poor

A2 social security benefits is the umbrella term for payments of this kind

A3 the state pension can be used to purchase anything whereas housing benefits can only be used for housing

A4 in-kind transfers do not require a direct transfer of income; rather, an individual can access a product free when others have to pay, e.g. school dinners

***examiner's* note** There is some debate about whether income transfers and transfers in-kind deal with market failure. Some argue that inequalities provide market signals that bring about an efficient allocation of resources. Others argue that redistributive policies raise economic welfare by transferring resources to areas of the economy that give rise to an overall increase in consumer satisfaction.

Government failure

Q1 Can government failure be measured?

Q2 Has government failed if it supplies a product that makes a loss on sales?

Q3 Identify two ways in which government can finance its expenditure.

Q4 An economist wrote: 'Governments find it difficult to exercise c............, to control the q............ of products and to m............ the workforce.'

Macroeconomics

Q1 How is macroeconomics distinct from microeconomics?

Q2 Which of the following areas of study is/are macroeconomic: the oil industry; changes in real GDP; changes in the rate of inflation?

Q3 Macroeconomics looks at the balance between a............ d............ and a............ s............ in an economy.

Q4 Identify two demand-side policies studied in macroeconomics.

ANSWERS

the study of economics at the level of the national and international economy

A1 microeconomics looks at smaller economic units, e.g. the consumer, the firm and the industry

A2 changes in real GDP; changes in the rate of inflation

A3 *aggregate demand*; *aggregate supply*

A4 fiscal policy and monetary policy, which can be used to manipulate aggregate demand

***examiner's* note** In economics there is no clear division between macroeconomics and microeconomics. There are two extreme areas of study: the consumer at the small scale and the world at the large scale. Beginning with the consumer, there are ever-larger aggregations that are studied by economists; and a somewhat arbitrary division is set between the industry and the national economy, as the dividing line between micro and macro.

Real GDP

Q1 Can GDP rise and real GDP fall?

Q2 What are the three ways of measuring GDP?

Q3 If nominal GDP is £1,017 billion in year 2 and the price index in year 1 was 103 and in year 2 is 105, what is the real GDP?

Q4 Do market prices or constant prices measure real GDP?

ANSWERS

the total monetary value of output
of an economy over a specified period,
adjusted for inflation

A1 yes, nominal GDP can rise as the result of inflation while the
    output of the economy falls

A2 using the aggregate of income, expenditure or output

A3 £1,017 billion $\times \dfrac{103}{105}$ = £997.6 billion

A4 constant prices — constant prices measure real output, while
    market prices include an element of price change

***examiner's* note** In AS economics it is most common to refer to the total
output of the economy using the real GDP measure. The less common measure
is GNP, which is GDP + net property income from abroad. However, it should
be recognised that GNP reflects all the income, including that from the
ownership of assets abroad, and therefore the spending power of the economy.
It is therefore a truer measure of the rewards from economic activity.

Productivity

Q1 What is the difference between production and productivity?

Q2 How is labour productivity measured?

Q3 Is it possible for productivity to increase and the output of the economy to decrease?

Q4 If the retail price index grows by 3%, GDP by 5% and the workforce by 4%, what has happened to productivity?

ANSWERS

a measure of output per unit of input into the production process

A1 production is a measure of output, while productivity is a measure of output per unit of input

A2 the physical output or the value of output of a firm divided by the units of labour used in the process

A3 yes, less can be produced even when there has been an increase in output per unit of input

A4 it is likely to have fallen by 2% (5% − 3% − 4%)

***examiner's* note** It is important to recognise that the calculation of labour productivity can be misleading, in that it assumes all output is determined by labour and does not take the productivity of other factors into account. A capital-intensive firm may have higher labour productivity than a labour-intensive firm purely because it uses more units of capital. Moreover, labour productivity could be increased by replacing labour with machines.

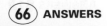

Standard of living

Q1 Can standard of living be measured by the income a person receives?

Q2 Is real GDP or the human development index (HDI) a better measure of living standards?

Q3 Is the standard of living likely to be higher or lower if wealth and income are more equitably distributed?

Q4 Which type of capital expenditure is not likely to improve future living standards?

ANSWERS ▶▶

a person's income, wealth and less
quantifiable characteristics, such
as stress levels and hours worked

A1 no, other characteristics can influence a person's living standard

A2 real GDP is a measure of the products available to people, while the HDI is a better measure of quality of life, including per capita income, life expectancy and literacy rates

A3 higher, as a more even distribution of income and wealth creates more overall satisfaction

A4 expenditure on military equipment and armaments

***examiner's* note** It is a common question to ask about the extent to which statistics such as GDP can measure and reflect differences in living standards between countries as well as changes in living standards over time in the same country. An understanding of living standards requires assessment of both quantity and quality aspects of human life and therefore involves a degree of value judgement.

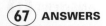 **ANSWERS**

Black economy

Q1 Give two examples of the functioning of a black economy.

Q2 Are tax avoidance and tax evasion part of the black economy?

Q3 Does a black economy increase or decrease the amount of trade that takes place?

Q4 Which pricing policy is likely to lead to the formation of a black market?

ANSWERS ▶▶

that part of an economy where trade is not recorded, often involving illegal transactions

A1 possible answers include: illegal drugs; gambling; prostitution; cash-in-hand employment

A2 tax avoidance is not, but tax evasion is part of the black economy

A3 it is likely to increase the total amount of trade that takes place in an economy

A4 if the price is set below a market-clearing price, shortages will exist and a black market may develop

***examiner's* note** A black economy will tend to develop where people perceive that there is excessive intervention by the state, which is not in their best interest. The black economy may or may not be legal. For example, it is illegal to sell certain drugs at present. However, it is not illegal to mow a neighbour's lawn for pocket money, although the activity is likely to go unrecorded in official trade statistics and is therefore judged to be part of the black economy.

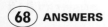

Aggregate demand

Q1 Identify the components of aggregate demand and the symbols used to represent them.

Q2 Which component comprises the largest proportion of aggregate demand?

Q3 Which component of aggregate demand is a balance between two totals?

Q4 Which two components of aggregate demand are not injections into the circular flow of income?

ANSWERS

the total nominal demand for goods and services from consumers, producers, government and foreigners

A1 consumption (C) + investment (I) + government expenditure (G) + (exports (X) – imports (M))

A2 consumer expenditure is greater than the sum of all the other components

A3 the balance in the AD function is X – M

A4 consumption is not an injection into the flow and imports is a withdrawal from the flow

***examiner's* note** In economics there are three levels at which demand is analysed: individual demand, market demand and aggregate demand. The component investment comprises two elements — the demand for capital, which is one firm depending on the output of another firm, and stock building which is, in effect, a firm demanding its own product. Stocks are necessary to guard against changes in demand.

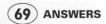

AD/AS model

Q1 What are the differences and similarities between AS_1 and AS_2?

Q2 Demand management will not be successful if the AS curve is which shape?

Q3 What levels of employment are achievable given (a) AS_1 and (b) AS_3?

Q4 How can a higher level of employment be achieved given AS_3?

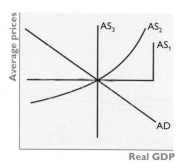

ANSWERS

uses aggregate supply and demand curves to explain macroeconomic equilibriums

A1 given AS_1 demand can shift and stimulate higher levels of employment without higher prices, whereas AS_2 trades off higher inflation and higher levels of employment; neither can expand past full employment

A2 AS_3; demand cannot manipulate real changes in the economy given this AS curve

A3 (a) full employment; (b) a natural level of unemployment

A4 the AS curve needs to be shifted right using supply-side policies

***examiner's* note** Economists agree on a single shape for the AD curve but disagree on the shape of the AS curve. Keynesian economists tend to support the shapes represented by AS_1 and AS_2 while monetarists tend to accept that the curve is vertical and adjustments to aggregate demand will only raise or lower the average level of prices. Policies to improve the level of employment and output require actions that shift the AS curve to the right.

Injections

Q1 Identify the three main injections into the circular flow of income and their representative symbols.

Q2 If government injected £1 million into the economy, would it raise GDP by £1 million?

Q3 Which of the injections into the circular flow is not determined from within the economy?

Q4 An injection into a fully employed economy is likely to raise n.............. GDP, but leave r.............. GDP unchanged.

ANSWERS ▶▶

autonomous additions of income into the circular flow

A1 government expenditure (G); investment (I); exports (X)

A2 because of the multiplier effect, GDP would be raised by more than £1 million

A3 exports, which are determined by demand in foreign countries

A4 *nominal* (through inflation); *real* (the real economy cannot expand further)

***examiner's* note** Any injection into the circular flow of income is likely to raise nominal (and usually real) GDP by a number greater than the original change. This is because the first round effect will raise income by the injection, but income flows from person to person and there will be subsequent changes that will raise GDP to a multiple of the original change. The extent of the final change will depend upon the value of withdrawals.

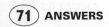

Withdrawals (leakages)

Q1 Identify the symbols for the three main withdrawals and match them to an injection.

Q2 Will withdrawals from the circular flow of income have a multiplier effect on GDP?

Q3 Which withdrawals are likely to increase as GDP rises?

Q4 As personal incomes rise, which withdrawal is most likely to show a greater increase in the proportion withdrawn?

ANSWERS ▶▶

A1 savings (S) match to investment (I); imports (M) match to exports (X); taxation (T) matches to government expenditure (G)

A2 yes, a downward multiplier effect

A3 all three withdrawals are likely to increase as GDP rises

A4 taxation, as its progressive nature increases the proportion taken away as incomes rise

***examiner's* note** A common mistake is to refer to exports as a withdrawal because they flow out of the economy. However, the income to pay for exports flows into the economy and the real flow should not be confused with the money flow. One problem that government faces when it tries to boost demand by reducing taxation is that individuals might spend their increase in disposable income on imports and therefore reduce the beneficial effect.

Gross domestic fixed capital formation

Q1 What does an economist mean by investment?

Q2 What is the difference between gross investment and net investment?

Q3 Capital depreciation can result from either d............... or o.................

Q4 For an economy to grow, is it necessary for gross or net investment to be positive?

ANSWERS ▶▶

the purchase of factories and machines — not to be confused with consumers buying investment products

A1 the buying of produced means of production, e.g. lorries, machines and factories

A2 gross investment is total investment, while net investment is total investment minus the value of capital depreciation

A3 *deterioration* (through wear and tear); *obsolescence* (through the development of more efficient alternatives)

A4 net investment must be positive, i.e. there must be more than enough investment to cover depreciation

***examiner's* note** The economist's definition of investment should not be confused with the everyday usage of 'investment' to mean the purchase of financial assets such as savings and investment products.

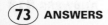

Government expenditure

Q1 Name two ways in which government expenditure is financed.

Q2 Identify two groups of products that are purchased by UK governments.

Q3 What is the difference between current and capital expenditure by government?

Q4 Rank the following areas of government expenditure in terms of the amount of money spent on them: social protection; defence; education; health.

ANSWERS

current and capital spending by government

A1 taxation and/or borrowing

A2 the most obvious groups are public and merit goods

A3 current expenditure is required to maintain the current level of services, while capital expenditure adds to the level of services

A4 social protection (including welfare payments) has the most money spent on it, followed by health, education and defence

examiner's **note** Economists generally agree that governments need to spend money on the public good, otherwise essential products, for which there is a collective demand, would not be available. There is more debate about whether merit goods need to be purchased on our behalf. This is because they are private goods with external benefits for society that are difficult to measure. In recent years, private individuals have been required to contribute more of their income to the purchase of education and health products.

Government taxation

Q1 Taxation is a w............... from the circular flow of income.

Q2 What is the difference between direct and indirect tax? Give an example of each.

Q3 What does the Laffer curve predict?

Q4 If a person's tax allowances are £5,000 and the first taxable band is 10% between £1 and £2,999, the second band is 25% between £3,000 and £19,999 and all additional income is taxed at 40%, how much tax is paid on an income of £27,000?

ANSWERS

taxes that individuals and organisations
are legally liable to pay in order to
finance government expenditure

A1 *withdrawal*

A2 direct tax is levied on income (income tax), while indirect tax is
levied on expenditure (e.g. value added tax)

A3 it predicts that at some point, as the income tax rate rises, the
total tax take will begin to fall as people avoid and evade tax

A4 £27,000 − £5,000 = £22,000 taxable income
(£2,999 @ 10% =) £299.90 + (£16,999 @ 25% =) £4,249.75
+ (£2,002 @ 40% =) £800.80p = £5,350.45

***examiner's* note** The prediction from the Laffer curve that, as income tax
rates rise, tax revenues will eventually fall is politically significant. If a country has
gone past the point of maximum tax revenue, there is a political advantage if tax
rates are lowered because the government not only gains votes by lowering tax,
but also gains more tax revenue and can thus gain even more votes by increasing
expenditure.

Government borrowing

Q1 What is the difference between the PSNCR and the national debt?

Q2 The government's borrowing requirement can be financed by b_____ old money or c_____ new money.

Q3 Is government borrowing usually related to expansionary or contractionary macroeconomic policies?

Q4 Treasury bills are usually sold to finance the mismatch between which two variables?

ANSWERS

the amount required to finance the gap between government spending and government revenue

A1 PSNCR is a yearly requirement, while the national debt is the accumulated debt built up over many years

A2 *borrowing*; *creating*

A3 borrowing is usually part of an expansionist strategy using a budget deficit

A4 revenue and expenditure

***examiner's* note** Short-term borrowing using Treasury bills recognises a difference between current spending and the flow of revenue to the Inland Revenue. However, as they are only 90-day bills, Treasury bills are not used to finance long-term borrowing. In recent years the Treasury has only borrowed long term to finance investment (the golden rule). However, this may be difficult to observe in the run-up to an election.

Unemployment

Q1 What is full employment?

Q2 Name five different categories of unemployment.

Q3 What is the natural level of unemployment?

Q4 What relationship was established by the Phillips curve?

ANSWERS

refers to any unused productive factor,
although commonly associated
with labour that is out of work

A1 Keynesian terminology for a level of employment where there are sufficient jobs available for those seeking work

A2 possible answers include: frictional; structural; disguised; demand-deficient; cyclical; casual; seasonal

A3 a level of unemployment, identified by some economists, that cannot be reduced in the long run by increasing aggregate demand

A4 rising levels of employment are related to rising wages and prices, while falling levels of employment are related to falling wages and prices

***examiner's* note** The unemployed are not homogeneous, so no single solution is likely to deal with unemployment. Solutions to demand-deficient unemployment will be different from solutions to frictional or casual unemployment. If people have decided that they do not wish to work and can live on benefits, the only solution to this type of unemployment is the politically difficult one of reducing benefits.

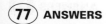

Claimant count

Q1 What is the other measurement of unemployment in the UK?

Q2 Explain how the claimant count could overestimate unemployment.

Q3 Explain how the claimant count could underestimate unemployment.

Q4 If the economy is at a level of full employment, would the claimant count be zero?

ANSWERS

A1 the Labour Force Survey, which estimates the total number of people currently seeking employment

A2 people claiming benefits could be working in the black economy

A3 there could be disguised unemployment, where people are not claiming benefits despite being unemployed

A4 no, some people would be in the process of changing jobs and some would be searching for employment

examiner's note The concept of full employment was a Keynesian estimate of the maximum number of people who could be employed through demand management before the economy became unstable in terms of rising prices. The concept is currently out of favour with economists, although the current (2004) high level of employment would have been registered as close to full employment in the years when there was a strong acceptance of Keynesian ideas.

Retail price index (RPI)

Q1 What is the difference between RPIX and RPIY?

Q2 What is a weighted retail price index?

Q3 What is the difference between RPI and HICP?

Q4 If the index numbers (and weights) for three products are 120 (3), 130 (2), and 97 (5), what is the weighted average index number?

ANSWERS

a measure of inflation and therefore changes in the value of money

A1 RPIX is the retail price index minus changes in mortgage interest rates, while RPIY also excludes indirect tax and council tax

A2 each item in the index is allocated a weight that represents the proportion of income spent on the product by the consumer

A3 RPI is the UK measure of inflation and is calculated arithmetically, while the harmonised index of consumer prices is the eurozone measure and is calculated geometrically

A4 $(120 \times 3) + (130 \times 2) + (97 \times 5) \div 10 = 110.5$

examiner's note RPI measures the average percentage change in a basket of prices. Weights are allocated to reflect the pattern of consumer expenditure. Over time, these weights change as new products are added and others removed and as the pattern of expenditure changes. The official measure for inflation in the UK is now the Consumer Price Index (CPI)

Inflation

Q1 Explain two causes of inflation.

Q2 What did Milton Friedman say caused inflation?

Q3 Can prices fall during a period of inflation?

Q4 Do debtors or creditors benefit during a sustained period of high inflation?

ANSWERS

a rise in the average (general) level of prices over a measured period of time

A1 • cost push (a rise in costs of production)
• demand pull (too much money chasing too few goods)

A2 the money supply growing at a faster rate than output

A3 yes, some prices can fall and the average can still rise

A4 debtors, as the real value of their debt falls and they have to pay back less in real terms

***examiner's* note** Demand-pull and cost-push inflation are terms used by Keynesian economists to explain the causes of inflation. Whereas Keynesian demand-pull inflation can occur only at full employment, monetarists say that inflation is always and everywhere a monetary phenomenon, and can occur at high or low levels of economic activity. Monetarists do not accept the cost-push cause of inflation.

Hyperinflation

Q1 What is the cause of hyperinflation?

Q2 What effect does hyperinflation have on the functions of money?

Q3 Persistent hyperinflation is likely to lead to a return to b................ .

Q4 Explain why some people have their wealth wiped out by hyperinflation while others do not.

ANSWERS

a high rate of inflation that leads to money being unable to function

A1 it is generally accepted that printing money is the only cause of hyperinflation

A2 money cannot function, or function properly, as a medium of exchange, unit of account, store of value or standard of deferred payment

A3 *barter* — the exchange of one product for another, which does not involve money

A4 wealth in the form of money is wiped out, while wealth in the form of property is not

***examiner's* note** Hyperinflation often starts in countries where the government is weak and resorts to printing money as a short-term expedient, rather than raising taxes. After the First World War, Germany printed money to pay for war reparations; the currency was later withdrawn and a new money was established.

Deflation

Q1 What is the difference between the deflator and deflation?

Q2 Which type of fiscal policy may lead to deflation?

Q3 Who benefits most from deflation: debtors or creditors?

Q4 What is a deflationary gap?

ANSWERS ▶▶

a fall in the average level of prices, or a reduction in the level of aggregate demand

A1 the deflator is a ratio of price indices used to remove the effect of inflation from national income statistics

A2 a budget surplus will reduce the expected level of aggregate demand

A3 creditors, as the real value of their savings increases

A4 it is used in Keynesian analysis to describe the difference between output at full employment and output at less than full employment

***examiner's* note** The two definitions of deflation have produced some confusion in economics. The most commonly used definition is a fall in the average level of prices, which is the opposite of inflation. The other definition of deflation — often used by Keynesians — is a fall in the aggregate level of demand, which can take place when the economy is experiencing inflation. By the second definition, inflation and deflation can occur at the same time — hence the confusion.

Unanticipated inflation

Q1 What is meant by the index linking of payments?

Q2 Why may unanticipated inflation cause a problem in the collective bargaining for wage rises?

Q3 Is unanticipated inflation likely to result in an expansion or a contraction in economic activity?

Q4 Unanticipated inflation can disrupt both consumer and producer e.............

ANSWERS

the actual rate of inflation minus the anticipated rate of inflation

A1 payments change under contract as a result of changes in the value of money

A2 wage agreements are often based upon the expected future rate of inflation

A3 it could lead to either, depending upon whether it was higher or lower than expected

A4 *expectations*

examiner's note The present action of producers, consumers and government is dependent, to a degree, on their expectations of the future rate of inflation. Some economists argue that unanticipated higher rates of inflation may cause a temporary rise in output as prices and profits rise while costs remain unchanged. This is then reversed when higher costs are incurred as a result of firms competing for scarce resources as they expand their business.

Costs of inflation

Q1 What effect will a higher rate of inflation have on a country's exchange rate?

Q2 Historically, does a low rate of inflation or a low rate of deflation have more damaging effects on an economy?

Q3 What is the difference between inflation and reflation?

Q4 If the retail price index rises from 100 to 120, what is the fall in the value of money?

ANSWERS 〉〉

inflation causes fluctuations in currency and interest rates and redistributions of income and wealth

A1 the exchange rate is likely to fall as revenues from exports fall and payments on imports rise

A2 a low rate of deflation has more damaging effects than a low rate of inflation, which can stimulate the economy

A3 inflation is a rise in the general level of prices, while reflation is an expansion in aggregate demand that may result in higher prices and/or higher output

A4 $(100/120) \times 100 = 83.3\%$ of its former value

***examiner's* note** As inflation rises faster, so the value of money falls quicker and people will reduce their active and idle money balances and make deposits into interest-earning accounts. Reflation may result in inflation, but an expansion in aggregate monetary demand can be absorbed by a growth in output without a rise in prices.

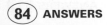

Expectations

Q1 What effect may an expectation of higher rates of inflation have upon consumers?

Q2 Give an example of how people's expectations before the chancellor's budget may change their actions.

Q3 What is the theory of rational expectations?

Q4 People take a view about the costs of acquiring information up to a point where the m........... c........... of the acquisition is equal to the expected future m........... b............

ANSWERS

what people anticipate will happen in the future and its impact on their current actions

A1 it may encourage them to bring forward purchases

A2 people may buy products before the budget if they expect their price will rise after the budget

A3 it assumes that individuals learn from experience and apply this learning to future events in the form of maximising behaviour

A4 *marginal cost; marginal benefit* (assuming rational consumers)

***examiner's* note** Expectations interest economists because expectations about future events influence current action, even when the expectation turns out to be incorrect. Consumers and producers both change current actions depending upon their ideas about future rates of inflation. Trade union wage negotiations are influenced by inflation forecasts. Economists need to take into account the fact that the current action is real, even if the future event does not materialise.

Economic growth

Q1 What is a production possibility boundary?

Q2 Using the diagram, what is the difference between growth of output and economic growth?

Q3 Producing which type of product is likely to boost economic growth?

Q4 What is the opportunity cost of producing more capital products?

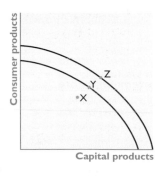

A1 it joins the different combinations of consumer and capital products that can be produced if the economy is working at full capacity

A2 X to Y is growth of output using unemployed resources; Y to Z is economic growth

A3 capital products

A4 fewer consumer products

***examiner's* note** Sustainable economic growth is important because, over the next 45 years, if the world economy grows at a modest 2.5% per year, its citizens will be three times better off than they are today. Economic growth offers the prospect of reducing poverty without having to make some people worse off. It also allows people to increase their leisure time and satisfies the expectations that people now have that their living standards will continue to improve.

Fiscal policy

Q1 What is the difference between the government's budget and fiscal policy?

Q2 Explain the term 'fiscal drag'.

Q3 What constraints are imposed on fiscal policy by the 'stability and growth pact' of the EU?

Q4 When will the government think of using a contractionary fiscal policy and what options are available to it?

ANSWERS ❯❯

using taxation/expenditure to manipulate aggregate demand and influence the level of economic activity

A1 the budget is usually a yearly event where government taxation and expenditure plans are laid out, while fiscal policy is using the budget to manage the level of overall aggregate demand

A2 fiscal drag is the restraining effect on a boost to aggregate demand caused by a rise in taxation through higher incomes and/or inflation

A3 the budget deficit should be no more than 3% of GDP and national debt no more than 60% of GDP

A4 when inflation is accelerating, the government will budget for a surplus to reduce aggregate demand

***examiner's* note** Governments have used budgets to manage aggregate demand, budgeting for a deficit to expand the economy and a surplus when the economy is overheating.

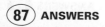 **87** ANSWERS

The Treasury

Q1 Who is the First Lord of the Treasury?

Q2 Which set of annual accounts is the responsibility of the Treasury?

Q3 The Treasury is ultimately responsible for government's s............ and t............ policy.

Q4 What is the Treasury model?

ANSWERS 〉〉

arguably the most important department
of the UK government in that it
manages macroeconomic policy

A1 the prime minister is the First Lord, not the chancellor of the
exchequer

A2 the annual budget statement, produced after listening to
representations from various government departments

A3 *spending; taxation*

A4 a computerised forecasting model used by the Treasury to
estimate future trends in the UK economy

***examiner's* note** The chancellor of the exchequer is the mouthpiece for an
enormous amount of work that goes on at the Treasury. Civil servants and
Treasury economists produce the government's overall expenditure plan and
decide how it is to be financed. The political party in power has some influence,
but not as much as politicians would lead us to believe.

Transfer payments

Q1 What is the role of transfer payments in managing the economy?

Q2 Identify two different transfer payments.

Q3 What is the difference between a transfer payment and a transfer earning?

Q4 What value do transfer payments have in the income measure of GDP?

ANSWERS ▶▶

payments usually made to an individual by government without the requirement of any productive effort

A1 they are used as part of the government's redistributive policy

A2 answers could include: various welfare payments; state pensions; student grants

A3 a transfer earning is that component of a factor reward that is required to keep the factor in its present use

A4 no value at all, as they are removed from the statistics to avoid double counting

***examiner's* note** There have been considerable changes in recent years in the way that governments use transfer payments. Welfare payments can easily become disincentives to work. State pensions will become increasingly difficult to finance as a greater proportion of the population lives beyond retirement age. Student grants are now more selective, as more students are entering higher education.

Monetary policy

Q1 Which two variables are manipulated in monetary policy?

Q2 What is meant by an accommodating monetary policy?

Q3 Which group within the Bank of England manages monetary policy?

Q4 What is the main target of monetary policy?

ANSWERS

using adjustments to interest rates and money supply to manage the economy

A1 the rate of interest and the quantity of money

A2 an accommodating monetary policy is dependent upon the targets set for fiscal policy

A3 the Monetary Policy Committee, established when the Bank of England became independent in 1997

A4 the Bank of England is given a target for inflation that was originally RPIX at 2.5% +/–1%, reduced to 2% as an HICP measure

examiner's **note** Since the Bank of England became independent, the emphasis of macroeconomic policy has been on a stronger monetary policy that imposes disciplines upon fiscal policy. Of the two variables available to the bank, interest rates have been, and remain, the focus of attention. Although it is possible to target the quantity of base money (cash) in the economy, this has never been seen as particularly important.

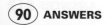

Supply-side economics

Q1 What is the difference between supply-side and demand-side economics?

Q2 When is taxation a supply-side rather than a demand-side policy?

Q3 What is the shape of the aggregate supply curve in models built by supply-side economists?

Q4 Give two examples of supply-side policies, excluding taxation.

ANSWERS

considers that solutions to macroeconomic problems are to be found on the supply side of the economy

A1 supply-side economics assumes no positive role for managing aggregate demand other than to maintain stable prices

A2 adjusting the tax structure and maintaining the tax take is a supply-side policy, whereas changing the balance of total taxation and total expenditure is a demand-side policy

A3 perfectly inelastic and therefore not responsive, except in terms of prices, to manipulations of aggregate demand

A4 possible answers include: deregulation; privatisation; reinforcing property rights; training and education; making markets more flexible

***examiner's* note** According to supply-side economics, the solutions to high unemployment and low economic growth are to be found on the supply side of the economy and not, as Keynesians suggest, from manipulating aggregate demand.

Demand-side economics

Q1 Identify two main problems that can be solved by demand-side policies.

Q2 The balance between which two variables is the focus of demand management?

Q3 Economists who accept the tenets of demand management assume the shape of the aggregate supply curve to be what?

Q4 How would demand-side policy cope with the twin problems of high unemployment and a large current balance surplus?

ANSWERS ▶▶

concerns itself with managing aggregate demand using fiscal and monetary policy

A1 possible answers include: inflation; unemployment; low growth; balance of payments problems

A2 government expenditure and taxation

A3 either perfectly elastic to the point of full employment or a normal, upward-sloping supply curve from left to right

A4 reflating aggregate demand will increase demand for domestic products and increase the demand for imports

examiner's **note** Managing aggregate demand using fiscal and monetary policy developed out of a Keynesian interpretation of the way an economy reacts to a particular stimulus. During the 1950s and 1960s the policy seemed highly successful as governments tried to fine tune economies to maintain high employment. The 1970s, however, produced reactions that did not support demand management, as increasing demand left both inflation and unemployment at unacceptably high levels.

Free trade

Q1 Which supranational organisation is concerned with promoting free trade throughout the world?

Q2 Which theory underpins the argument for free trade?

Q3 What is a free trade area and how does it differ from a customs union?

Q4 Why is the infant industry argument used against free trade and for protection?

ANSWERS

non-intervention by governments in the
flow of imports and exports across
international boundaries

A1 the World Trade Organization (WTO)

A2 the theory of comparative advantage, which assumes that all
resources are allocated under a condition of free trade

A3 a free trade area is a group of countries which trade freely with
each other, but maintain their own barriers against the rest of the
world; a customs union is similar, but has a common external tariff

A4 infant industries are trading under the disadvantage of not having
reached their long-term optimum size

examiner's note Theoretically capitalism, market forces and comparative
advantage allocate resources efficiently and maximise the real GDP of every
country in the world. In reality, individual countries do not always perceive this
and erect barriers to protect themselves against other countries, producing a
complex trading model.

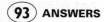 **93** ANSWERS

Exports

Q1 In order to buy the exports of another country, it is first necessary to buy the c............ of that country.

Q2 Are export subsidies a protectionist device?

Q3 Is the demand for exports likely to increase or decrease if the external value of the currency falls?

Q4 If a change in the exchange rate increases the demand for exports, what determines whether export sales revenue will also increase?

ANSWERS

A1 *currency*

A2 yes, they protect domestic industry by increasing the competitiveness of the product in foreign markets

A3 increase — export prices will fall and therefore demand will rise

A4 the elasticity of demand for exports will need to have a value greater than 1

***examiner's* note** It is a common error to assume that an increase in demand and therefore supply of exports will automatically improve the current account of the balance of payments. This may be so if the demand for exports has shifted to the right, or if the demand has increased as a result of a fall in domestic prices when the demand for exports is elastic. If demand for exports is inelastic, then a fall in price and an increase in sales will be accompanied by a fall in revenue.

Imports

Q1 Is it possible to consume an imported product in its country of origin?

Q2 As imports come into the country, are they recorded as a positive or negative flow on the balance of payments?

Q3 What is an import tariff?

Q4 Why may countries pursue a policy of import substitution?

ANSWERS

goods and services produced abroad
but consumed by residents
of the domestic economy

A1 yes, a holiday abroad is an imported product

A2 a negative flow, as the direction of the payment for the imports
is out of the country

A3 a tax on an imported product

A4 a policy of producing domestically what is currently being
imported may be pursued to stop money leaving the country

***examiner's* note** Countries have sometimes tried to become self-sufficient
and reduce imports to an absolute minimum, e.g. China in the middle of the
twentieth century. The policy has not been successful, as it goes against the
theory of comparative advantage. Today China is very much involved in
international trade and, arguably, growing much faster as a result. Imports begin
to become a problem when their value significantly exceeds the value of a
country's exports.

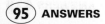

the difference between the value of total payments into and out of a country over a specified period

A1 strictly, a balance is a difference between two totals; it tells us nothing about the totals

A2 no, it is only correct to refer to a deficit on a component of the account, as the overall balance is always zero

A3 a significant imbalance, either a deficit or a surplus, on a component of the balance of payments

A4 goods and services; the former is usually in deficit, the latter in surplus

examiner's note A restructuring of the accounts in 2000 produced three significant subdivisions: the current account; a new capital account, which only includes transactions in fixed assets; and a financial account, which is similar to the old capital account. Any deficit or surplus that remains after accounting for the current balance, capital balance and unofficial flows on the financial account is offset by official financing to produce a zero balance.

Balance of payments

Q1 What is meant by the word 'balance' in 'balance of payments'?

Q2 Is it correct to refer to a balance of payments deficit?

Q3 What is meant by a disequilibrium in the balance of payments?

Q4 Which two accounts comprise the current balance? Are they usually in deficit or surplus?

ANSWERS

Current balance deficit

Q1 Trade in services is in surplus +£87m, trade in goods is in deficit −£112m and the financial account is in surplus +£38m. What is the current balance?

Q2 Referring to Q1, what is the balance on the capital account?

Q3 Over the long term, which account on the balance of payments has most influence on the external value of the currency?

Q4 On which account is the purchase of shares in foreign companies and the receipt of dividends recorded?

ANSWERS ▶▶

the value of exported goods and services is less than the value of the corresponding imports

A1 a deficit of £25m, as the balance on the financial account is not included in the current account

A2 to produce an overall zero balance the capital account is −£13m

A3 the long-term trend is determined by what happens on the current account

A4 purchase of shares is recorded on the financial account, receipt of dividends on the current account

***examiner's* note** The current balance deficit is the shortened description of the balance of payments current account deficit. Over the long term it is the most meaningful account. It is the national account into which flows of income are received and from which payments are made to other countries. Imbalances on this account illustrate the long-term economic viability of a country and its relative strength in the trading world.

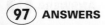 **97** **ANSWERS**

Protected trade

Q1 What is the difference between a tariff and a quota?

Q2 Identify two reasons acceptable to economists for raising a protective barrier around an economy.

Q3 Is consumer welfare improved by protectionist policies?

Q4 How does the CAP protect EU farmers from international competition?

ANSWERS

restrictions are placed on imports and help given to exports to protect industry from foreign competition

A1 a tariff is a tax on an import, while a quota is a limit on the volume of an import

A2 possible answers include: dumping; unfair competition; infant industries

A3 it is likely to be worsened as consumers will be paying higher prices and have restricted choice

A4 by variable import levies up to the agreed minimum guaranteed price

***examiner's* note** Politically, protectionist policies are difficult to manage effectively. The introduction of protectionist measures is likely to lead to retaliation from other countries, so negating the anticipated advantage. Moreover, once a protective device has been put in place, it will tend to have an immediate advantageous effect on votes, but it will subsequently be difficult to remove because of the damaging effect that its removal will have on votes.

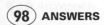

Tariff

Q1 Distinguish between a specific tariff and an ad valorem tariff.

Q2 In the diagram, which equilibrium exists in the absence of international trade?

Q3 Which equilibrium exists given free international trade?

Q4 Given free international trade, what effect will a tariff have upon domestic supply and imports?

ANSWERS ▶▶

a tax on imports that gives a competitive edge to domestic producers

A1 a specific tariff is a nominal amount on each unit imported, while an ad valorem tariff is a percentage of the price

A2 P_3Q_3 will clear the domestic market

A3 P_1Q_5 where OQ_1 is produced domestically and $OQ_5 - OQ_1$ is imported

A4 it will increase domestic production from OQ_1 to OQ_2 and reduce imports from $OQ_5 - OQ_1$ to $OQ_4 - OQ_2$

***examiner's* note** Tariffs distort markets and, although they offer a measure of protection to domestic producers, they disadvantage the domestic consumer. This diagram is an important one to learn, as it can be used to compare internal with international trade as well as trade with and without tariffs. The significant point to recognise is the effect on domestic production and imports as price changes.

Dumping

Q1 Is a country dumping its product in other countries if the price it charges is significantly lower than its competitors because of cheap labour costs?

Q2 Does the EU dump surplus agricultural products on the world market?

Q3 What is meant by the statement 'dumping often involves the compliance of government'?

Q4 Explain how tariffs and quotas can be used against dumping.

ANSWERS

A1 no, this is the action of competitive market forces, although it may raise an issue about labour exploitation

A2 yes, because the product has its price lowered by a variable export subsidy

A3 essentially dumping is a loss-making exercise and firms cannot continue to do this without financial help from a third party, often government

A4 tariffs can be used to raise the price of the dumped products, while quotas can be used to limit their supply

***examiner's* note** All forms of dumping are considered to be unfair competition. The aim of dumping may be to break into new markets, destroy competition, maintain domestic prices and clear surpluses, or prevent new firms from being established. In reality, it is difficult to identify dumping, as the evidence is not easily found.